W9-CFB-859

J
612.8
BJO

Bjorklund, Ruth

The senses

THE SENSES

RUTH BJORKLUND

mc Marshall Cavendish
    Benchmark

Marshall Cavendish Benchmark

99 White Plains Road

Tarrytown, New York 10591

www.marshallcavendish.us

All websites were available and accurate when this book was sent to press.

Editor: Karen Ang

Publisher: Michelle Bisson

Art Director: Anahid Hamparian

Series Design by: Kay Petronio

Library of Congress Cataloging-in-Publication Data

Bjorklund, Ruth.

The senses / by Ruth Bjorklund.

p. cm. -- (The amazing human body)

Includes bibliographical references and index.

Summary: "Discusses the parts that make up the human senses, what can go wrong, how to treat those illnesses and diseases, and how to stay healthy"--Provided by publisher.

ISBN 978-0-7614-4043-7

1. Senses and sensation--Juvenile literature. I. Title.

QP434.B56 2010

612.8--dc22

2009020877

 = nerve cells responsible for transmitting sensory signals

Front cover: Hearing, smell, and taste are some of the human senses.   Back Cover: The three ear bones.

Photo research by Tracey Engel

Front cover photo: J. Bavosi / Photo Researchers, Inc.

The photographs in this book are used by permission and through the courtesy of: Getty: DEA Picture Library, 4; Tomek Silkora, 6; 3D4 Medical.com, 9, 16, 21, 56; Ryan McVay, 11; Dorling Kindersly, 12, 15, 45; Dr. Richard Kessle & Dr. Gene Shih, 14; Nucleus Medical Art.com, 18, 27, 38, 43; UHB Trust, 20; Dennis Kunkel Microscopy, Inc., 23; Doug Struthers, 24; Gregor Schuster, 26; Dr. Fred Hossler, 28, 29, 53; Dr. John D. Cunningham, 31, 54; Cathy Crawford, 44; Howard Huang, 47; Ron Levine, 58; Darryl Leniuk, 60; John Cumming, 61; Phil Boorman, 62; Peter Cade, 64; Ewa Ahlin, 65; Tim Platt, 66; Dougal Waters, 68; Jutta Klee, 69.Photo Researchers, Inc: Susumu Nishinaga, 10, 30; Omikron, 22; Steve Gschmeissner, 32; BSIP, 35; ALIX/Phanie, 40; John Bavosi, 48; PHANIE, 50; Will & Deni McIntyre,51.

Printed in Malaysia

123456

CONTENTS

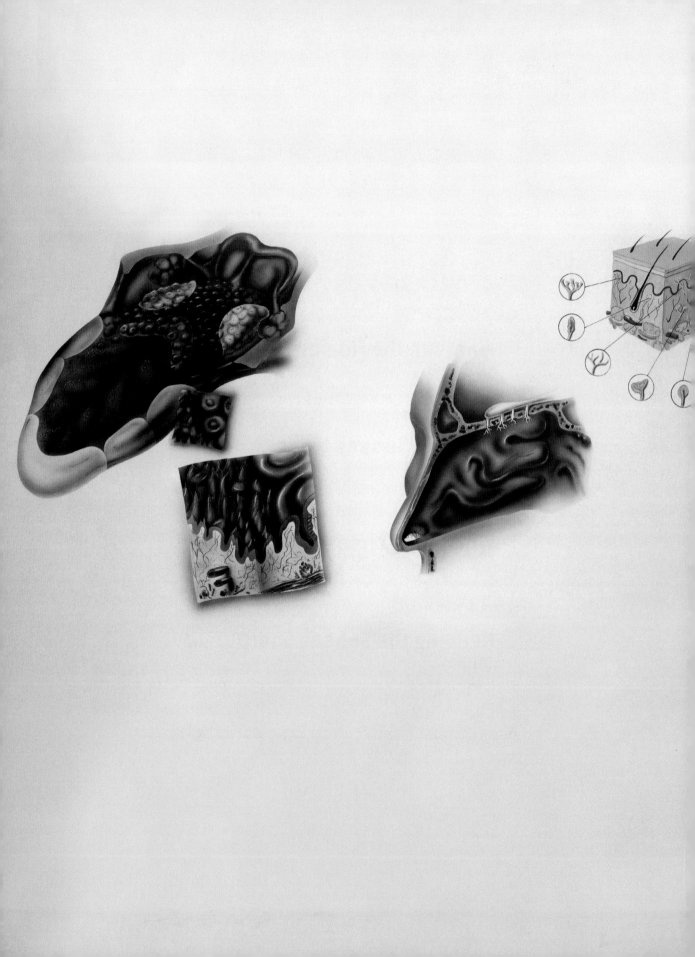

1

What Are the Human Senses?

he human senses are what people use to gather information and understand the world around them. Traditionally, it has been determined that there are five senses—sight, smell, touch, taste, and hearing. More recently, however, experts have also added another, called proprioception, or an awareness of the body in space.

Sense organs recognize changes in the environment. These changes are called stimuli. Specialized cells called sensory receptors convert the stimuli into impulses that are carried by a network of nerves to the spinal cord and to the brain. Each sense organ has a

An illustration shows three of the human body's senses—taste, smell, and touch.

specific path to the brain. Sensory information is processed in specific areas inside the brain.

SIGHT

Sight, or vision, is one of the most important and frequently used senses. The human brain is constantly being bombarded with visual input from its surroundings. The portion of the brain that interprets the sense of sight is larger than all of the other portions of the brain devoted to the other senses. Several different types of vision receptors in the eyes contribute to the brain's ability to process visual information. Eyes contain receptor cells that receive information about light, shape, and color. The receptor cells deliver that information to the visual cortex area of the brain. Visual nerve impulses travel quickly from the eyes to the visual cortex directly through the optic nerve, located behind each eyeball.

The iris, which is a ring of colored muscle, is one of the most noticeable parts of the eye.

The eye is a complex organ with many specialized parts and layers. The eye is delicate and is protected from injury by the skull and eyebrows, and is kept clean by eyelids and eyelashes. The eyeball is a sphere about an inch in diameter. It is held in place inside the eye sockets of the skull by small muscles. These muscles are called extra ocular muscles and allow the eye to move up and down and side to side. On the outside of the eyeball is white protective layer of fibrous tissue known as the sclera, or the white of the eye. The sclera keeps the eyeball's round shape. At the front of the eye is a curved, clear, rounded membrane called the cornea. Behind the cornea is a chamber filled with fluid that is called the aqueous humor.

The eye has a round circle of tiny muscles called the iris. The iris has pigment and can be green, hazel, brown, or blue, giving the eye its color. The iris surrounds a tiny hole called the pupil. Most of the time, the pupil does not look like a hole because it glints in the light. But what is seen as the "sparkle" in the eye is actually a clear, finely layered flexible lens. It can be seen by looking through the hole that is called the pupil. Tiny fibers hold the lens in place and connect it to eye muscles called ciliary muscles. Behind the lens, most of the rest of the eye is filled with a thick jelly-like fluid called the vitreous humor.

Covering 65 percent of the lining of the back of the eye is a thin, light sensitive layer called the retina. The retina itself has many layers—photosensitive cells called rods and cones that pick up light and color, bipolar cells which convert light into electrical impulses, and ganglion cells that form nerve fibers to transmit signals to the brain. Closest to the back of the eyeball is a single cell layer that contains pigment. Its purpose is to absorb light and prevent it from bouncing back through the eye once it has reached the retina. Vision is clearest at the center of the retina in an oval, yellowish area called the macula, or macula luteus. And at the center of the macula is an area known as the fovea.

Nerve fibers form bundles at the back of the eye. The bundles come together at the optic disk, or "blind spot" and pass out of the back of the eye to a large nerve called the optic nerve. The left and the right side optic nerves cross behind the eye and meet at an area called the optic chiasma. Nerve signals travel back to the areas in the brain where vision is processed—the thalamus, brainstem and visual cortex.

HEARING

After the sense of sight, the sense of hearing is the most developed sense in the human anatomy. The ear is a precise and efficient organ that performs its sensory duties in a compact area. The ear is comprised of three main parts—the outer ear, the middle ear, and the inner ear. The visible part of the ear is called the pinna (sometimes also called the auricle) and is made up of folds of cartilage covered in skin. At the base of the pinna is the lobule, or ear lobe. The pinna surrounds an opening called the external auditory canal. This is a one-inch tube that tunnels through a bone in the skull known as the temporal bone. This tube is lined with tiny hairs, oil-producing sebaceous glands, and sweat glands called ceruminous glands, which produce earwax, or cerumen. As sound waves move down the external auditory canal, they come upon the final portion of the outer ear, the temporal membrane.

Beyond the temporal membrane is the middle ear. The middle ear is made up of three tiny bones, which are the smallest bones in the body. Collectively they are called the ossicles and individually they are known as the malleus, incus, and stapes. Their more common names come from their shape—the hammer, anvil, and stirrups. Both the outer ear and the middle ear are filled with air, while the inner ear is filled with fluid. Between the middle ear and the inner ear are two membranes, called the oval window and the round window.

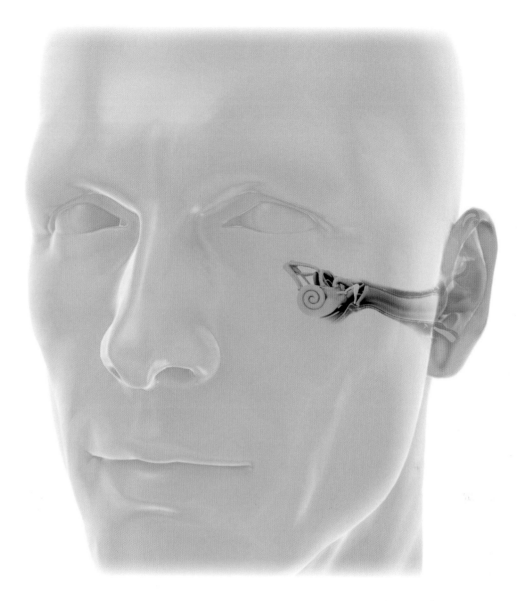

The human ear is made up of external parts located outside of the head, and a collection of tiny internal parts inside the skull.

The inner ear, or labyrinth, has three winding chambers deep inside the temporal bone of the skull. The front part is the cochlea, which is a coiled chamber that holds the organ of Corti. The organ of Corti is a mass of tiny hairs that are the sound receptor cells. The vestibule chamber, which contains sensory cells related to balance—the utricle and the saccule—connects the cochlea to the final chamber, the semicircular

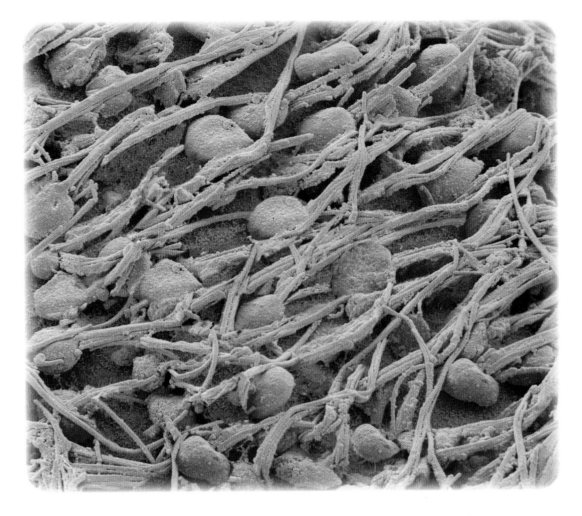

Special hairs, called cilia, and other cells found in the inner ear help with hearing and balance.

canals. Nerve signals leave the ear and travel to the brain through the vestibulocochlear nerve. This nerve is actually two nerves, the cochlear nerve, which transports information about sound, and the vestibular nerve that delivers information about balance.

PROPRIOCEPTION

The fifth sense, proprioception, or equilibrium and balance, is managed by sensors in the ear. Often called the vestibular system, the semicircular

Structures in the inner ear and brain allow a person to balance, stand upright, move, and perform athletic activities.

canals and the vestibule region sense movement, speed, and stasis (the state of being still). The semicircular canals exist at right angles to each other. At the base of each of the canals lies a widened duct called the ampulla. Inside each ampulla is a jelly-like mass called the cupula. This mass contains hair cells that are attached to nerves. As fluid called endolymph circulates in the canals and vestibule it stimulates receptor cells. In the vestibule, the utricle and saccule sense movement and action of the head.

TASTE

The sense of taste, or gustation, as it is also known, determines not only the flavor of food, but also provides an awareness of whether or not something put in the mouth is safe or good to eat. There are five basic tastes, one of which was not agreed upon in the scientific community until only recently. The tastes are salty, sweet, sour, bitter, and *umami*. *Umami* was established by a Japanese scientist named Kikunae Ikeda. He wrote about *umami* being a taste that responds to glutamate,

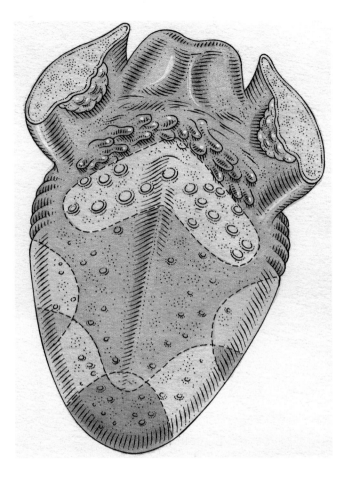

The different parts of the tongue are responsible for various taste sensations.

a chemical found in foods, such as bacon, corn, mushrooms, tomatoes, some seaweed, fish, and other foods.

The taste organ is a collection of specialized cells called taste buds. There are approximately 10,000 taste buds found on the top of the tongue, and more found in the throat, soft palate (soft tissue found at the back of the roof of the mouth), and the epiglottis (the flap of cartilage at the base of the tongue). Each taste bud bears between 50 to 150 sensory taste receptors. Along the top and sides of the tongue are various small bumps called lingual papillae.

There are four types of papillae, three of which contain taste buds. On the sides of the tongue are the foliate papillae, which appear as a series of ridges. Fungiform papillae are small, rounded projections found all over the tongue, especially at the tip and along the top of the sides. Each of this type of papilla contains up to five taste buds. There are only five to twelve of the largest papillae, called the circumvallate papillae, but they contain more than 250 taste buds each. They form a "V" shape near the back of the tongue. The fourth type of papillae, filiform papillae, are found all over the tongue and though they are the most numerous, they do not carry any taste sensors.

A nerve called the facial nerve carries sensory information from the taste receptors in the front of the tongue. The glassopharyngeal nerve carries information from the rear of the tongue. A third nerve, the vagus nerve, carries information from the back of the mouth. These nerves deliver taste sensations to part of the brainstem, then travel on to the thalamus, and finally arrive in the cerebral cortex of the brain.

SMELL

The olfactory sense, or sense of smell, is a powerful sense. The human nose can detect thousands of distinctly different odors. The sense of smell identifies odors in the air around us and assists the sense of taste by enhancing or discouraging appetite and contributing to the appreciation or the rejection of flavors. It also protects us from breathing unsafe air or fumes and stops us from eating anything spoiled or poisonous. The sense of smell also helps with human memory recall.

There is a large cavity located between the roof of the mouth and the bottom of the skull called the nasal cavity. It is divided into left and right sections by a piece of cartilage called the nasal septum. Inside each side of the nasal cavity are three bony shelves folded with ridges called conchae.

The conchae create passageways for air to travel before entering the respiratory tract.

The nasal cavity is lined with a membrane that contains mucus-producing cells. On the uppermost part of the nasal cavity is a layer of tissue called the olfactory epithelium. On one end of each olfactory cell are long hairs called cilia. The cilia are coated in mucus and contain sensory receptors. At the other end of each olfactory cell are nerve endings called axons. The axons of the olfactory cells come together to form the olfactory nerve. The nerve passes through the skull and enters the end of

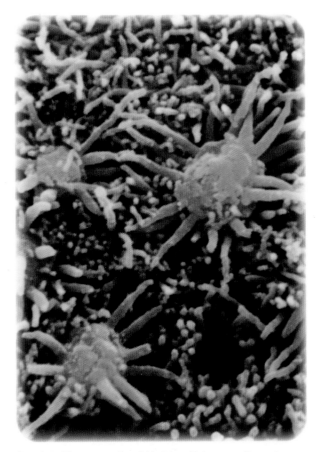

Special olfactory cells aid in identifying smells and other information that comes in through the nose.

the olfactory tract, where a pair of olfactory bulbs is beneath the front of the brain. Inside the olfactory bulbs, nerve cells receive signals and transfer them to parts of the brain.

TOUCH

The sense of touch involves a wide network of nerve endings and sensory receptor cells. There are three overall types of receptor cells—visceral cells, which are cells found in internal organs, somatic, which are found in joints and bones, and cutaneous, which are found in the skin. The skin, the largest organ of the body, contains most of the sensory receptors for touch.

It is itself composed of several layers. The visible top layer of skin is called the epidermis and it provides protection for the layers of skin below and also protects the rest of the body. Of the many types of cells found in the epidermis, very sensitive touch sensors provide information to the brain. The second layer is a thick layer containing sweat glands, hair follicles, oil glands, blood vessels, nerve endings and touch receptors. There are four basic types of touch receptors: mechanoreceptors, thermoreceptors, pain receptors, and proprioceptors. Each is responsible for recognizing different types of sensation, such as pressure, pain, or temperature.

Nerves beneath our skin allow us to feel things and use our sense of touch to react to and interact with the environment.

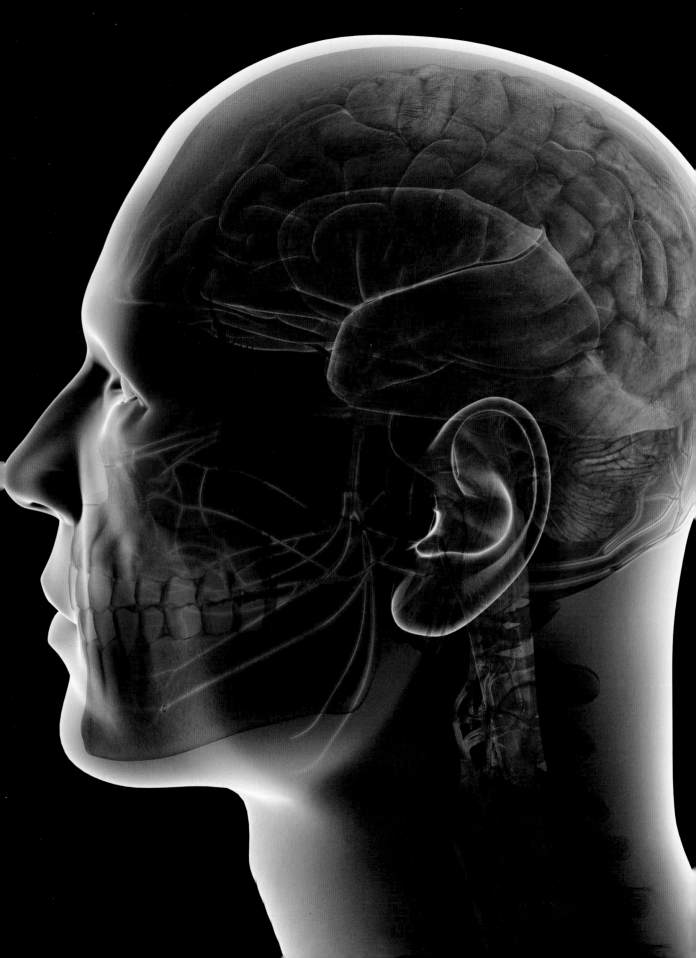

2

How the Senses Work

Many different organs and body parts work together to form the human senses. Sometimes more than one sense rely on the same structures.

VISION

Everything the eye sees comes from reflected light. In other words, the eye cannot view an object unless some form of light shines on the object. As light hits the object and bounces off, it travels in the form of light waves. These waves of light enter the eye through the cornea.

The brain and the rest of the nervous system process all of the sensory information that is delivered by the sensory organs.

Anatomy of the Eye

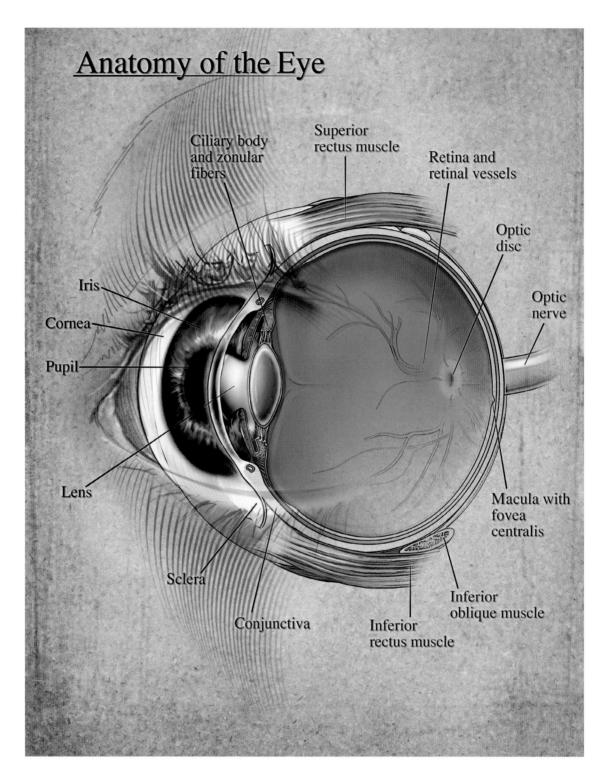

The cornea slows down the speed of light. It is curved, causing the cornea to bend the rays of light toward each other. The process of bending light rays is known as refracting light.

The refracted light waves move through the aqueous humor and pass through the pupil toward the lens. If the light is very bright, the muscles of the iris relax, decreasing the size of the opening of the pupil, and letting in less light. The iris also reduces the size of the opening of the pupil when the eye is trying to concentrate its focus on an object that is close by. Conversely, if the light is dim, or if the eye is viewing an object in the distance, the iris muscles contract. This dilates, or opens up, the pupil, to let in more light.

The lens of the eye is extremely flexible. It is able to focus on an object that is just inches away, but is equally able to quickly adjust to viewing a distant planet in the sky. Bright light travels to the cornea in ever-widening waves. However, the cornea can bend the rays only so far. The lens must further refract the light in order to focus properly. The lens is composed of more than 2,000 fine layers called lamellae. As the light passes through each layer, the rays of light are bent in tiny degrees of refraction. When the eye focuses on closer objects or is receiving bright light, the muscles holding the lens relax causing the lens to become more rounded. The rounder the lens, the greater its ability becomes to refract light. On the other hand, light coming from a more distant source travels toward the eye in an almost parallel pattern. The eye does not need to refract light to the same degree. As a result, most of the refraction in this instance can be done by the cornea. The muscles holding the lens contract and flatten the lens. Light passes through nearly unchanged.

After light has been focused by the lens, it passes through the vitreous humor. The thick liquid retains the sharp focus of the refracted light and ushers the light toward the retina at the back of the eye. The retina receives the refracted light rays and turns them into electrical impulses that are fed to the brain. The retina is covered in arteries and veins and is an uneven surface. Some areas of the retina are more light sensitive than others and are better able to perceive images with greater sharpness, or acuity. Arteries and veins bypass the most light-sensitive area of the retina, which is called the fovea. To achieve the most acute vision, light must fall on the fovea. However, light enters the eye from many directions, so the eye must compensate in order for light to be directed to the fovea. Eyes do so by constantly moving up and down and

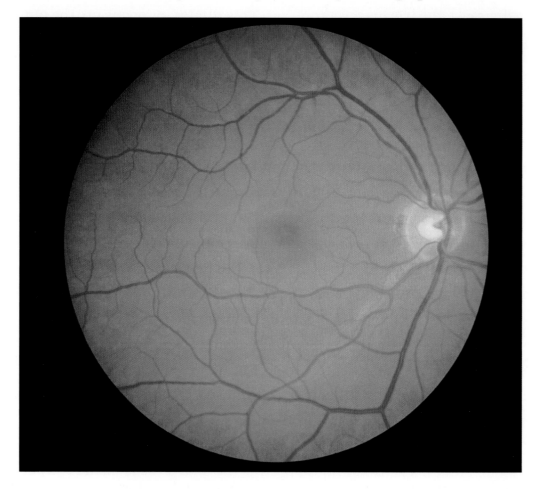

The retina has many blood vessels traveling across its width.

Rods and cones (right) are located along the retina at the back of the eye.

side to side. There is also a blind spot in the retina, called the optic disk. It is the point where the optic nerve fibers meet and travel out of the eye.

The retina, or sensory tunic, has two layers. Closest to the back of the eyeball is a single cell layer that contains pigment. Its purpose is to absorb light and prevent it from bouncing back through the eye once it has reached the retina. The neural layer of the retina contains sensory receptors and other nerve cells that help process light signals. Closest to the vitreous humor are the bipolar cells and ganglion cells. Light passes through these cells, bending the light ever so slightly toward the sensory receptor cells of the retina, known as rods and cones.

Rods and cones can only be seen using a microscope. The rods have been colored blue in this micrograph.

Most rods are found beyond the macula, around the periphery of the retina. Rods are shaped like tiny cylinders. They are filled with disks of purple pigment, which contain molecules of chemical receptors and proteins that respond to dim light. When bright light falls on a rod, the pigment becomes bleached and cannot respond to the stimuli. In bright light or daylight conditions, the rods do not function. But when in darkness, the rods recover from the "bleaching" effect after 10 or 15 minutes and are able to provide vision in dim light or near darkness. Consider walking from bright light into a dark room. It takes a few minutes for eyes to adjust to seeing in the reduced light.

Cones are shaped like upside-down triangles. They need bright light to react to stimuli. Cones contain pigments—red, yellow, and blue. Each color responds to different wavelengths of light. More cones are found in the macula, and only cones, and not rods, are found in the fovea.

Rods and cones react to the light and send a signal through a synapse to bipolar cells. A synapse is a point of connection between two neurons, or nerve cells. Neurotransmitters, or chemical messengers, travel across the synapses between neurons. Bipolar cells then excite ganglion cells. Ganglion cells have long tails called axons. When these axons are bundled together they form nerves that penetrate the back of the eye at the optic disk and extend through the optic nerve and into the brain. Impulses from the ganglion cells are called action potentials.

There are approximately 1.5 million ganglion cells in the human retina and more than 100 million photoreceptors (rods and cones). There are more rods than cones. There is a concentration of cones in the macula and the fovea. In the fovea for example, there may be just a single cone sending signals to five ganglion cells. However, on the periphery of the

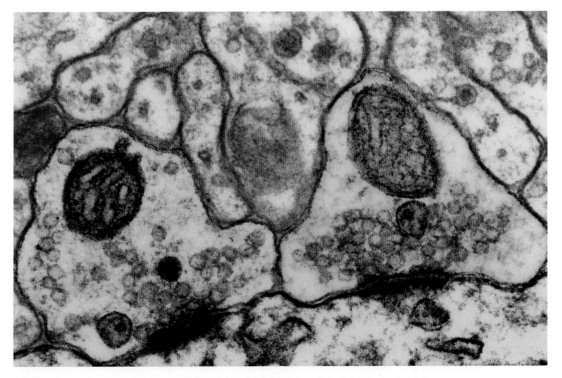

Nerve receptor cells are responsible for receiving and sending sensory messages.

retina, beyond the macula, there may be thousands or more photoreceptor cells sending impulses to one ganglion cell.

Photoreceptors become excited by light and stimulate the bipolar cells behind it. But before the next phase is completed, the rods and cones also excite additional cells called horizontal cells. Horizontal cells prevent some of the neighboring bipolar cells from sending signals. So ganglion cells do not receive signals of equal strength, but rather receive signals in a pattern of lines, contours, shading, and shapes. Ganglion cells also receive color and brightness information with varying degrees of hue and intensity.

Action potentials travel through nerve fibers through the back of the eye into the optic nerve. Visual impulses coming from the right eye and impulses coming from the left eye meet in a location behind the eyes called the optic chiasma. Some of the impulses travel to the brainstem,

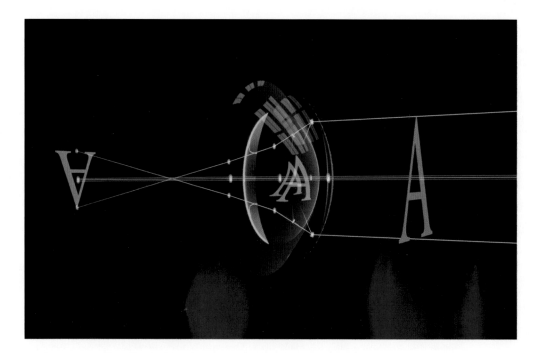

Images first entering the eyes and heading toward the brain appear upside down(left). The brain turns the images right side up when it processes them for you to understand.

where one area determines how much the pupils must dilate or narrow. Another area, called the superior colliculi, controls eye movement.

Most visual impulses, however, pass through the thalamus deep in the brain to the visual cortex. The thalamus separates visual information into color input and motion input before the information is processed by the visual cortex. The brain receives information from the two eyes and turns it into three-dimensional images. The images are transmitted to the brain upside down. The brain turns them right side up. The brain must also associate the image with previous experience to assess the incoming information. In other words, the brain must know "green" before it can label an object green, it must know that a face contains eyes, nose, and mouth in order to see a face. It will also fill in missing or confusing information to create a whole image.

HEARING

Sound is made up of molecules in air, water, and solid objects that vibrate and create waves of pressure. To make a sound, molecules vibrate and then bump into other molecules, which also begin vibrating. This continues so that sound vibrations travel outward. Sound travels in waves of different lengths and frequency.

The human ear responds to a greater amount of stimuli than any of the other senses. The ear has the ability to discern a range of sounds from near silence to blasts of explosive noise. The ear understands sound in two measurements, pitch and loudness. Pitch, or tone, is the sense of whether the sound is high or low. It is measured by the frequency of sound waves, that is to say, how often wavelengths travel past a given point. As each wavelength passes the point, it is called a cycle. The frequency is measured as cycles per second, or hertz (abbreviated Hz). The audible range of human hearing is from 20Hz to 20kHz (kilohertz, which is equal

Sound waves can be recorded and measured to gauge their strength.

to 1,000 Hz). The human ear is more sensitive to frequencies similar to the range of speech, 500 Hz to 4kHz.

Loudness is measured in terms of decibels, abbreviated dB or db and named after the inventor of the telephone, Alexander Graham Bell. A single decibel, or 0 dB, is considered to be the faintest sound audible to the human ear. Each rise in decibel is ten times louder than the last. A whisper is usually 15 to 20 dB, normal conversation is 60dB, and 130dB is often called the threshold of pain. Standing next to a jet airliner as it starts up would be a painful and intolerable 140 dB.

Sound waves travel all around us. Some flow directly into the ear, and others are gathered by the pinna and directed into the auditory canal.

Anatomy of the Ear

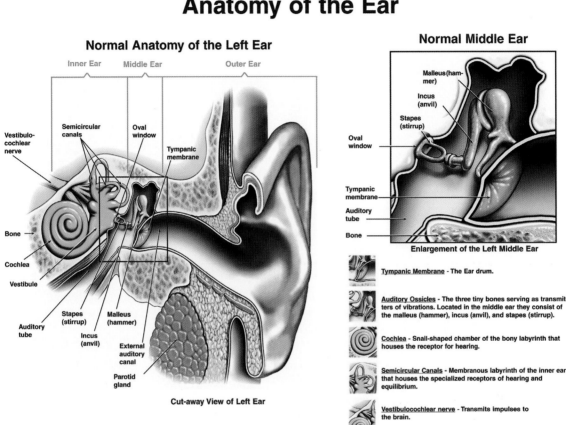

Normal Anatomy of the Left Ear

Inner Ear   Middle Ear   Outer Ear

Vestibulo-cochlear nerve

Semicircular canals

Oval window

Tympanic membrane

Bone

Cochlea

Vestibule

Auditory tube

Stapes (stirrup)

Incus (anvil)

Malleus (hammer)

External auditory canal

Parotid gland

Cut-away View of Left Ear

Normal Middle Ear

Malleus (hammer)

Incus (anvil)

Stapes (stirrup)

Oval window

Tympanic membrane

Auditory tube

Bone

Enlargement of the Left Middle Ear

<u>Tympanic Membrane</u> - The Ear drum.

<u>Auditory Ossicles</u> - The three tiny bones serving as transmitters of vibrations. Located in the middle ear they consist of the malleus (hammer), incus (anvil), and stapes (stirrup).

<u>Cochlea</u> - Snail-shaped chamber of the bony labyrinth that houses the receptor for hearing.

<u>Semicircular Canals</u> - Membranous labyrinth of the inner ear that houses the specialized receptors of hearing and equilibrium.

<u>Vestibulocochlear nerve</u> - Transmits impulses to the brain.

The vibrations pass across the cilia in the canal and reach the concave surface of the tympanic membrane, or eardrum. The eardrum vibrates and passes the vibrations through to the ossicles in the middle ear. The ossicles, the tiniest bones in the body, knock into each other in a chain reaction. The first ossicle—the malleus, or hammer—is attached to the tympanic membrane. Attached to the malleus is the incus, or anvil, which is also connected to the stapes, or stirrups. The stapes is attached to the oval window, which is the entrance of the inner ear. Because one side of

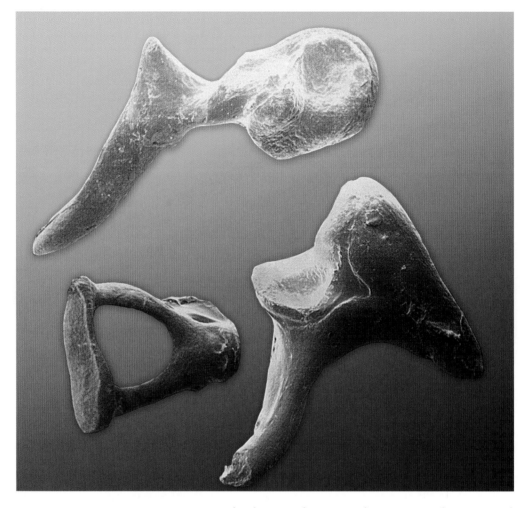

The three bones of the middle ear: the incus (top), stapes (bottom left), and malleus (bottom right).

the oval window is filled with fluid, more force is needed to pass the sound vibrations into the inner ear. The movement of the ossicles amplifies the vibrations coming from the outer ear and transfers the sound to the inner ear. If the sound is too deafening, however, tiny muscles attached to the eardrum and ossicles contract and reduce the vibrations.

Deep in the temporal bone of the inner ear are the receptors for the senses of hearing and equilibrium. Inside the bony labyrinth of the inner ear are three passageways. One, the cochlea, is responsible for the sense of hearing. It is shaped like a snail shell and contains three fluid-filled chambers. The center chamber holds the organ of Corti, which contains three outer rows with tens of thousands of hair cells and one inner row containing more than 3,000 hair cells. Each hair cell varies in length and has nerve fibers at its base. Depending on the pitch and loudness of the sound, certain hair cells in the inner row respond and become excited by the vibrations. The vibrations are converted into nerve signals. The nerve signals pass along nerve fibers to the cochlea nerve, which runs through the organ of Corti. The signals are then relayed to the brain stem, the thalamus, and then to the hearing sector of the temporal lobe of the brain.

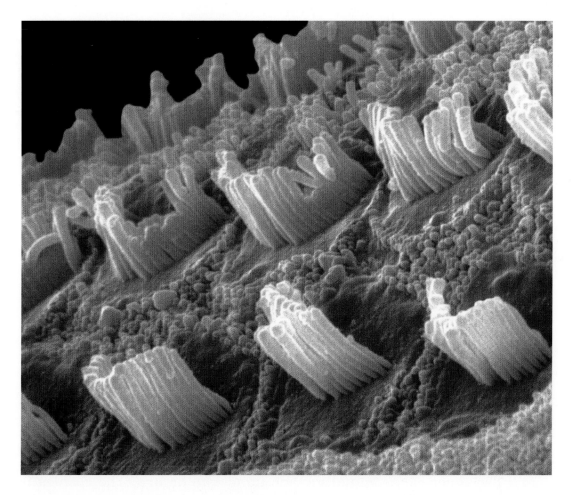

Hairlike cilia line the different parts of the inner ear.

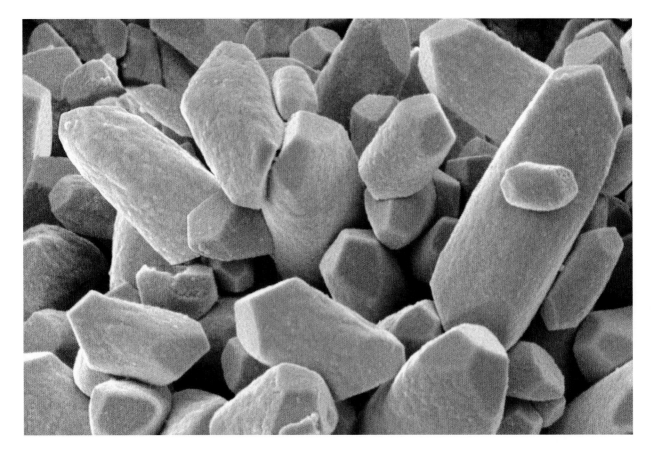

Crystal-like rocks in the inner ear help with balance.

PROPRIOCEPTION

Proprioception is the ability to sense position, location, orientation, balance, and movement of the body and all its parts. Proprioceptors are special nerve endings found in muscles, tendons, joints, organs, and the inner ear. These sensory receptors respond to stimuli inside the body that react to the body's position, movement, or speed. For example, even if your eyes are closed, you can still be aware of the location of your hands or feet. The sense of balance is based on gravity, rotation, and acceleration.

The inner ear is actually made up of two organs. The cochlea is responsible for hearing and the vestibular organ is responsible for balance. Sensory receptors in the vestibular organ are located in three areas—three semicircular canals, the utricle, and the saccule. Lying next to the cochlea are the three semicircular canals, which are filled with fluid. They receive information about the movement and position of the head. The ends of the canals touch the utricle. The utricle detects the head moving side to side and it touches the saccule, which detects when the head is moving up and down. Signals created in each are sent to the vestibulocochlear nerve, also called the auditory nerve, through the skull and into the brain.

TASTE

Taste is part of the sensory mechanism that guards the body and helps it experience its surroundings. The sense of taste is actually a mixture of sensations, taste (gustation), smell (olfaction), and touch (tactile). Taste receptors are located on taste cells that are clustered together in groups called taste buds. They are found on the front, sides, and back of the tongue,

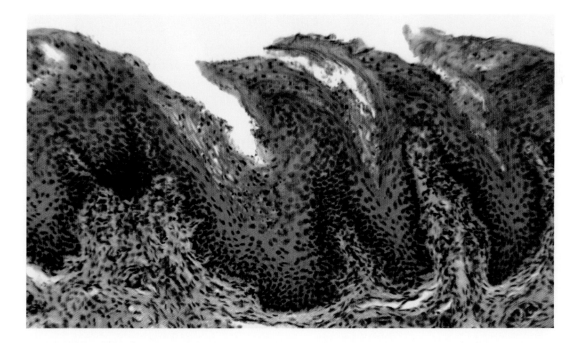

A magnified image shows papillae on the tongue.

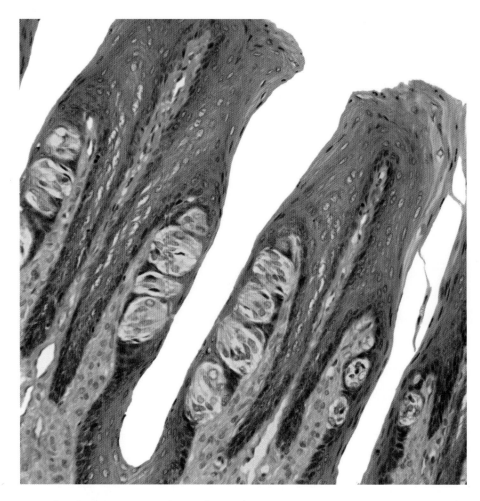

The papillae (red) have many taste buds (yellow) on them.

the mouth, and the larynx. Taste buds sit on pillar-like projections called papillae. There are four types of papillae, and three of them contain taste buds.

Each taste bud holds 50 to 150 taste cells. Small hairs called microvili are attached to the taste cells. Microvili contain the sensory taste receptors. Most taste receptors are chemoreceptors, which means they respond to chemicals that enter the mouth. When a substance enters the mouth it brings chemicals that will bond to the taste receptors. As the receptors are stimulated by the chemicals, they convert the chemicals into nerve signals, or action potentials. Inside each taste bud is a network of taste nerves. There are three pathways that the taste signals travel to reach the brain. One leads from the front and sides of the tongue, another from the back of the tongue, and the other from the mouth and larynx.

There are receptors for each flavor inside of each taste bud, so the taste nerves deliver a complex variety of taste signals to the brain. For example, tasting an apple can deliver a message that it is both sweet and sour. When tasting something, the first taste signals are more intense than the signals that follow. So the first bite of a peach is distinctly sweet, but the nerve signals adjust to the sensations. The brain becomes accustomed to the sensation and subsequent bites seem less flavorful than the first.

Each general flavor has importance. Sweet sensations usually mean that the substance is high in energy nutrients, umami delivers the taste

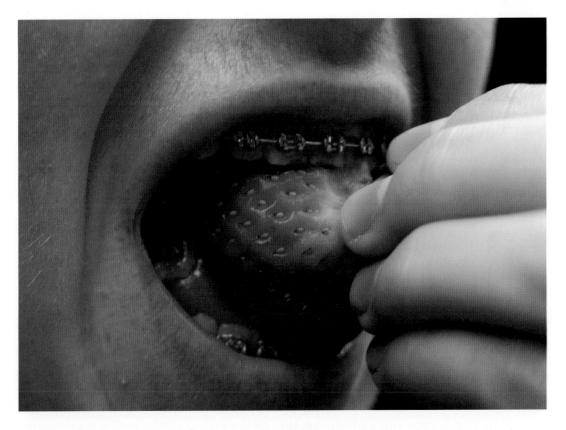

Sweet tastes, like ripe strawberries, are made possible by taste receptors on the tongue.

of amino acids which are proteins, salt helps regulate body fluids, sour is usually the flavor of foods high in acids, and bitter tends to represent toxins of various strength. There are also upper limits of taste that the body can tolerate. Some tastes are so related to touch sensors that they are not classified under one of the five tastes. Some of these include spicy (such as hot pepper), dryness (such as an unripe banana or grape), or coolness (such as spearmint).

Other receptors that serve the sense of taste respond to temperature and touch. Some foods gain or lose their desirability based on these stimuli. Receptors that respond quickly to a very hot drink, for instance, help protect the body. They sense that the drink is too hot and decrease the drink's desirability. Touch receptors, called mechanoreceptors, respond to texture in food—for example, creamy, crunchy, watery, or chewy. Some foods are pleasing more for their texture than taste, such as buttered noodles. In China, foods that have virtually no flavor are nonetheless highly prized for texture, such as bird's nest soup, which tastes bland but feels jelly-like. This phenomenon is called "mouthfeel."

SMELL

Like the sense of taste, the sense of smell, or olfaction, is a chemical sense. Olfactory chemoreceptors respond to odor-bearing chemicals in the surrounding environment. Olfaction is an ancient sense, in that early humans relied heavily on this sense for survival. For these people, their sense of smell could immediately alert them when a situation was dangerous. Olfaction is also the first sense to fully mature and develop in human infants—well before vision and hearing. Scientists have discovered that as an infant grows, the first way it recognizes its mother is by scent.

In the upper part of the nasal cavity lies the olfactory epithelium, where a mucus-coated membrane captures odor-bearing chemicals. Hair

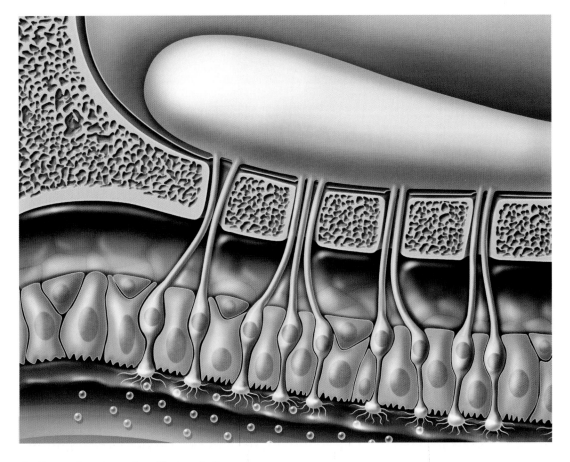

An illustration shows the olfactory bulb.

cells called cilia have olfactory receptors on one end and nerve fibers or axons on the other. Humans have about five million olfactory nerve cells and about 40 million olfactory receptors. The axons send the electrical impulses to the olfactory bulb. The bulb transmits the signals directly to the olfactory cortex. From the olfactory cortex, signals are distributed to the hippocampus, amygdala, and hypothalamus, which are parts of the limbic system. The limbic system of the brain contributes to memory and emotional behavior. Scientists continue to study how smell and memory are related. Because the olfactory areas of the brain are next to the areas of the brain that store memory and experience emotion, the two areas influence one another.

SMELLS AND MEMORIES

Many studies have shown that smells can bring back old memories and stored up emotions with greater intensity than remembered images or sounds. Scientists have studied the relationship between smell and memory. In one experiment, Swedish doctors from the University of Stockholm studied people age 75 and older. The scientists encouraged the participants in the study to describe the earliest memories they could recall. They showed the participants old photographs to help them remember and played music that was popular when they were younger. These cues helped the people remember periods of time dating back to their teenage and young twenties, but no further and with little detail.

However, when the experimenters introduced particular odors, such as old roses, fresh baked bread, or kitchen spices such as cardamom, the participants' memories improved. With odors as memory cues, the participants could recall their childhood years, from when they were as young as ten years or less. The older people vividly described events and emotions from long ago. The scientists concluded that the sense of smell can help a person maintain memory and emotions throughout a lifetime. They hoped to use their studies to aid older people with problems associated with age and memory, such as dementia, Alzheimer's, and other forms of memory loss.

TOUCH

Besides sweat glands and blood vessels, the dermis, or bottom layer of the skin, holds hair follicles and nerve endings that help provide the sense of touch. Tissues and organs deep beneath the skin also contain sensory receptors. Sensory receptors can be mechanical, thermal, or chemical. The receptors on nerve endings can detect pressure, pain, and temperature. Some parts of the body are more sensitive than others. Sensory receptors called Meissner's corpuscles respond to light touch. They are usually found in hairless areas such as the fingertips, tongue, eyelids, lips, and palms. Paccinian corpuscles are receptors deep in the bottom layers of the skin. They respond to the sensation of pressure and vibration, itchiness, warmth, and cold.

Pain

The most numerous receptors in the skin respond to pain. Receptors that reside on nerve fibers that respond exclusively to pain are called nociceptors. One type of nociceptor responds to sharp, fast pain. These nerve fibers are wrapped in a membrane called a myelin sheath. The sheath allows the nerves to transmit signals at a rapid pace. Nociceptors found on nerves that do not have a myelin sheath—called unencapsulated nerves—respond to dull, aching pain. The signals from these nerves travel much slower.

There are two main types of pain—somatic and visceral. Somatic pain is a result of nociceptors being stimulated in the skin, muscles, joints, bones, tendons, and ligaments. Visceral pain is produced by nociceptors that are found in internal organs and body cavities. Examples of these cavities and organs include the thorax, which contains the heart and lungs; the abdomen, which contains the liver, kidneys, spleen, stomach, and intestines; and the pelvic cavity, which holds the bladder and reproductive

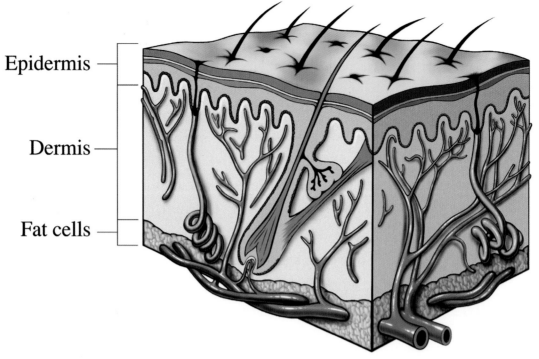

Skin protects the body, but also provides us with sensory information we need to function.

organs. There are fewer nociceptors in these areas than in the skin and soft tissues.

Temperature

Sensors on the skin and within the body also respond to the sensations of heat, cold, texture, and pressure. Temperature is important because the body must regulate its heat in order to stay healthy. Many of these sensors are on the tongue. This prevents a person from swallowing foods or drinks that are too hot. Sensors in the face and chest respond to cold in order to protect vital organs within. The ability to sense textures and pressure allows the body to accurately hold, grab, and lift, as well as to pull away or push against objects.

The Science of Haptics

An airline pilot operating the controls of an airplane feels a pressure and a vibration when using the flight instruments. The pressure or vibration sends a quick message alerting the pilot that something about the plane requires attention. But modern controls are electronic, and there are no mechanical levers or springs that would provide the sensation of pressure or vibration. Instead, these sensations are simulated by the technology called haptics. Anyone who has felt a cell phone vibrate or used a game controller has experienced haptic technology. Researchers in the field study how the human sense of touch works and apply those principals to their inventions.

An important advance in human health comes from the study of haptics for robotic prostheses, or artificial body parts. Successful treatments have been performed on people who have lost an arm. A prosthetic device is attached at the shoulder or elbow where the arm had been removed. Nerves in the shoulder or elbow that once controlled the missing arm still are able to communicate with the brain. To make use of this connection, the arm nerves are re-routed to a patch of skin on the chest. Nerves already in the skin of the chest are cut to create numbness and lack of feeling. Then the arm nerves from the severed limb are placed in the area to grow. Sensory receptors in the new nerves deliver information about the missing arm to the brain. With therapy, the person learns to stimulate the sensory receptors in the chest and the tactile center of the brain to deliver and transmit messages to and from the prosthetic arm. People using these devices say that when someone touches the special area on their chest, it feels as if their original hand was being touched.

Haptic scientists have also developed training programs for medical students learning surgical techniques with a computer simulation program. They have added applications so that students not only see the virtual surgery they are performing, they can also "feel" it. In another example of a haptic application, researchers are developing means for online shoppers to inspect merchandise by haptic interfaces, such as feeling the texture of fabrics, experiencing the fit of a baseball glove or the feel of a musical instrument, or the swing of a golf club.

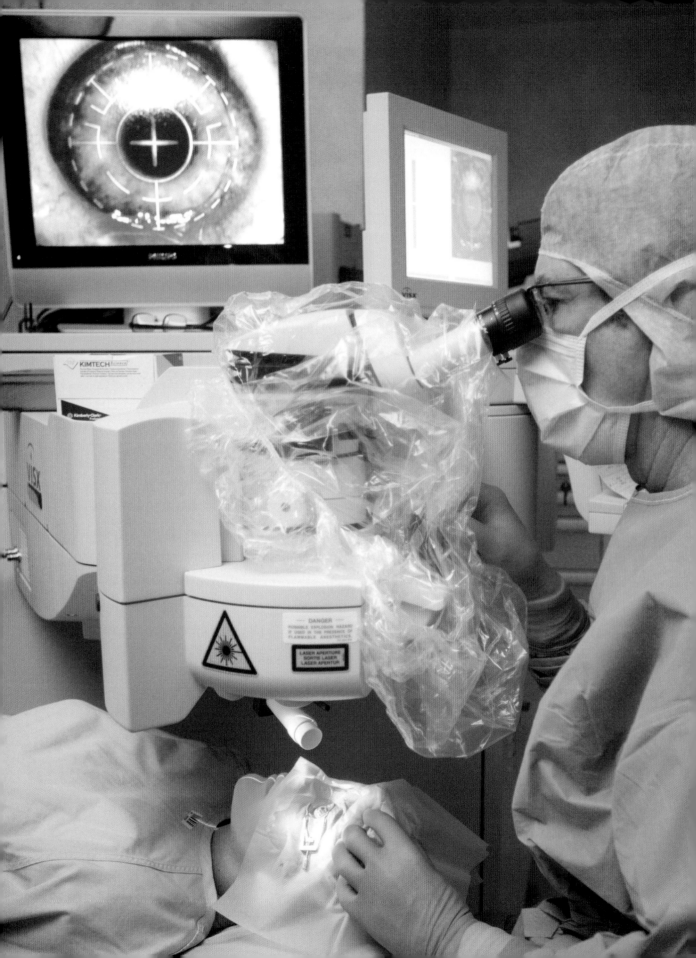

3

When the Senses Fail

The different senses allow people to navigate the world around them. The senses can fail, however, causing damage and danger to the body.

VISION IMPAIRMENT AND LOSS

Some vision disorders affect the optical part of the eye, such as the eyeball or lens regions, the muscles of the eye, the retina, and the visual cortex of the brain. Most common disorders affect the lens. When a baby is born, the size of the eyes and the skull continue to grow. If the

Laser procedures are often performed to fix vision or other eye problems.

eyeball does not keep up with the growth of the skull, the eyeball becomes too long and the lens and retina cannot work together well. This condition is called nearsightedness, or myopia, and objects are blurry when viewed from a distance. If the eyeball becomes too short, focusing is also blurred, causing farsightedness, or hyperopia. A person who is farsighted can see distant things better than objects that are close. More people are farsighted than nearsighted.

Under most conditions, eyeglasses, contacts, or Lasik surgery corrects these problems. During Lasik surgery lasers are used to change the shape of the cornea so that the eye is able to focus better. After Lasik surgery, many people find that they no longer need glasses or contact lenses to improve their vision. However, this surgery does not correct all vision problems for all people.

Another condition, called presbyopia, develops in some people forty years old and older. Protein changes in the lens of the eye cause the eye to become stiff, making it hard to focus on nearby objects. Presbyopia is usually corrected by glasses with bifocal or trifocal lenses. Bifocal lenses improve vision for distance and close-up. Trifocals also corrects for seeing middle distance.

Other conditions that affect the tissues of the eyeball are astigmatism and cataracts. People with astigmatism have corneas that are misshapen and prevent accurate focus. Often, this can be corrected with eyeglasses, and sometimes with soft contact lenses. A cloudiness that forms on the lens is called a cataract and usually occurs as the eye ages. To restore vision, surgery is often performed to remove the lens and replace it with an artificial lens.

Injury or trauma to eye muscles can diminish vision. The most common trauma, strabismus, known also as "lazy eye," tends to occur mostly in young children. The muscle that pulls the eye from side to side becomes damaged and the eye drifts toward the nose. The signals that are

Cut section of
the eye

Normal lens
(transparent)

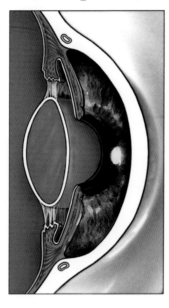

Lens clouded
by cataract

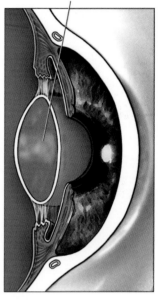

Cataracts often form as a person ages. If caught early enough, some forms of treatment can be used to help people with cataracts.

sent to the brain by the lazy eye are unclear. Without treatment, the brain may ignore the incoming signals and simply process the signals from the other eye. This condition is called amblyopia. Amblyopia is serious and can lead to a total loss of vision in the affected eye. Glasses and sometimes surgery are used to repair this condition. However, more often—especially in children under the age of seven—an eye patch placed temporarily over the healthy eye will cause the weaker one to strengthen.

Vision impairment or loss can also occur in the neurons and nerves of the eye. The neurons found in the back of the eye are quite

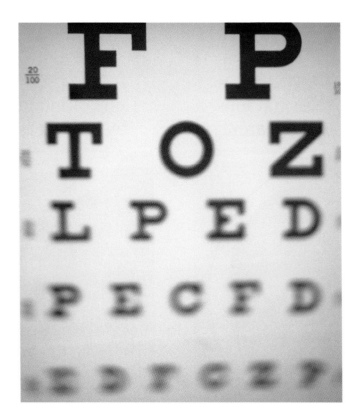

Vision tests usually include charts that gauge how well your eyes focus with and without glasses or contact lenses.

delicate and can easily be damaged. A genetic, or inherited, disease of the retina is called retinitis pigmentosa. Rod cells disintegrate so that the eye loses vision on its periphery and in dim light. Macular degeneration is another retinal disease, often occurring in older people. Cells are lost in the macula—the area surrounding the fovea—where vision is sharpest. As these cells fail, focusing becomes blurry and eventually this condition can lead to blindness. Rod cells in the retina can lose the ability to detect images in dim light, a condition known as nightblindness. Glaucoma is another serious condition, in which a buildup of pressure in the eye damages the optic nerve. Surgery, laser treatments, and prescription eye drop medications can help prevent vision loss due to glaucoma.

Vision impairment or loss can also come from the area of the brain that processes visual input—the primary visual cortex, located in the occipital lobe in the back of the brain. A severe blow to the head can cause a concussion that damages the visual cortex. When this happens, the eye and the nerves function normally, but the brain is unable to process the visual signals it receives. Strokes and tumors can also affect the brain's ability to process vision, recognize color, or follow objects in motion.

Colorblindness

Cones are the color sensitive receptors on the retina. Each cone has a pigment that responds to one of three colors, red, blue, or green. Cones combine their visual sensitivity to create all the variety of color we see. Sometimes there can be missing cones or there can be cones with less pigment affecting the way the retina perceives color. The inability for a person to see certain colors is called colorblindness. Males are more likely to be colorblind than females.

All people with colorblindness have defects that affect green and red sensitive cones. Rarely are blue cones affected. Contrary to what many may believe, a person with color blindness does not simply see everything in black, white and grey. Rather, greens and reds are distorted and thus when mixed together and with blue, colors take on muted and less varied hues. Though some people may not distinguish at all between red and

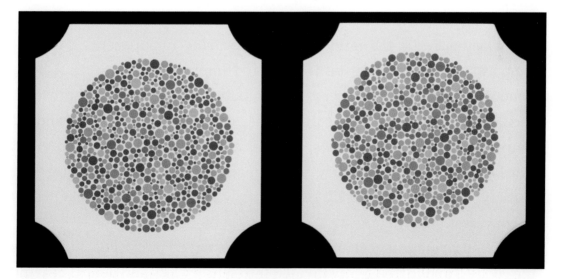

This is part of a test eye doctors use to determine whether or not a person is colorblind.

green, that condition is very rare. People with colorblindness often adapt very well and find ways to compensate for their condition. Sometimes people with colorblindness can even see details that normal-sighted people miss.

A form of colorblindness called protanomaly refers to a weakness in seeing red. A person with this form of colorblindness will see a shade of purple as being no more than another shade of blue because the red involved in seeing the color purple is lacking. Deuteranomaly, a weakness in perceiving green, affects some men. Other forms of colorblindness cause individuals to be unable to distinguish between red, orange, yellow, and green shades.

HEARING IMPAIRMENT AND LOSS

Hearing loss can occur from birth or later in life due to injury, serious infection, exposure to very loud noises, or an extreme build up of inner ear fluid. Less than 5 percent of Americans experience hearing impairments and fewer still experience total hearing loss. There are three general types of hearing impairments: conductive, sensorineural, and mixed hearing loss. Conductive is the mildest form of hearing impairment, it can be temporary and can often be treated and improved with medical help. Conductive hearing loss occurs in the outer or middle ear. It prevents people from hearing low or soft sounds, such as vowels. Understanding conversation at normal levels can be difficult. Often, a hearing aid can be fitted to help amplify sound reaching the ear. Speech reading therapy, sometimes called lip reading, may also be used to assist people in conversation with others.

Sensorineural hearing loss, sometimes called presbycusmis, affects the cochlea and is frequently divided into sensory loss and neural hearing loss. Sensory hearing loss affects the sensory receptors found on the tiny

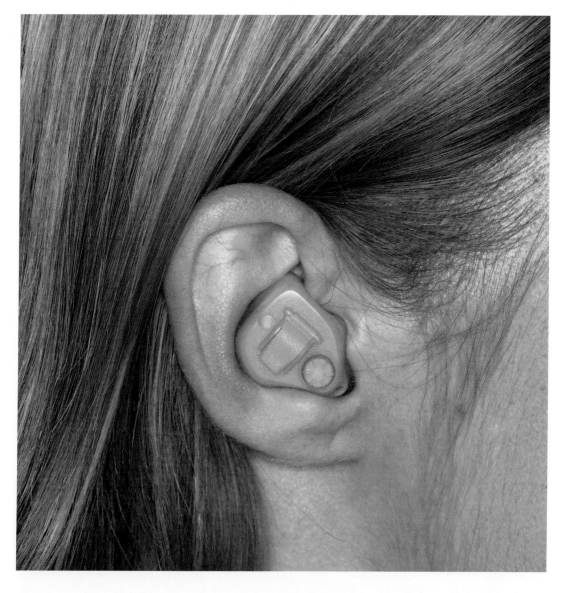

Hearing aids can help to amplify and direct sounds. Today, hearing aids come in many shapes and sizes—some are so small that you can barely notice them.

hairs in the cochlea. Damage to the hairs interferes with the nerves' ability to transmit signals. Sound becomes muffled, sometimes to the point of producing no sound at all. A person who has this condition may not hear speech well enough to imitate sounds and may as a result have difficulty in speaking.

Neural hearing loss describes the connection between the cochlea and the brain. Signals from the cochlea do not reach the brain correctly, or at all. Loud noises, such as loud machinery or listening to loud music through headphones, infections such as meningitis, and excess fluid in the ear all can damage the cochlea. People with neural hearing impairments may be able to hear very loud noises but the signals reaching the brain are distorted. Sometimes a hearing aid can help. Cochlear implants can be put in during a complicated surgery. A cochlear implant is a small electronic

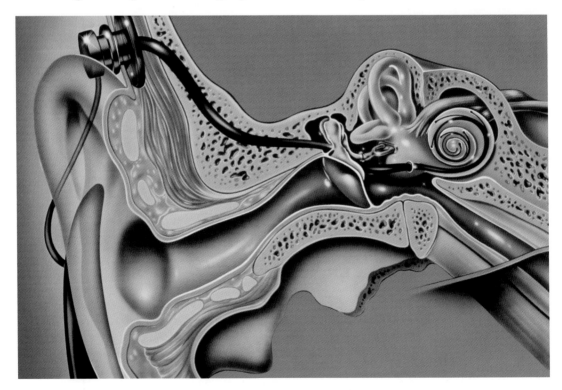

This illustration shows how a cochlear implant is positioned inside and out of the ear.

medical device that is placed in the ear and enables a person with hearing loss to experience a reasonable semblance of sounds. The device has a microphone, a processor and the ability to send electric signals along the pathway to the brain.

A person with mixed hearing loss will have a combination of sensorineural and conductive impairments. This disorder generally creates substantial hearing loss. Nerves leaving the ear, the brainstem or the hearing processor in the brain can also suffer damage leading to hearing loss.

Four categories describe types of hearing loss. Mild hearing loss means that a person cannot hear soft sounds. With moderate hearing loss, a person does not hear speech at normal levels. A person with severe hearing loss will not hear speech and few loud sounds. Profound hearing loss means that a person will not hear speech and few, if any, very loud sounds. There are approximately 20 million deaf or hearing-impaired persons in the United States. Many develop hearing loss as older adults. Only about 4 percent of hearing impaired persons have a hearing loss at birth.

Communication for the Hearing Impaired

There are five basic strategies for those with hearing impairments to develop good conversational skills and language understanding. One strategy is a complete language of its own. Others are "building blocks" to conversation and language learning. Those that develop a hearing loss at birth or before age five are more likely to learn American Sign Language (ASL) or Conceptually Accurate Signed English (CASE). Those who develop hearing loss after age five are more likely to have learned to form sounds and to communicate verbally. People who can speak will generally make use of one of the building blocks to learning language and assist in conversation.

Audiologists use special equipment to test the hearing in both ears.

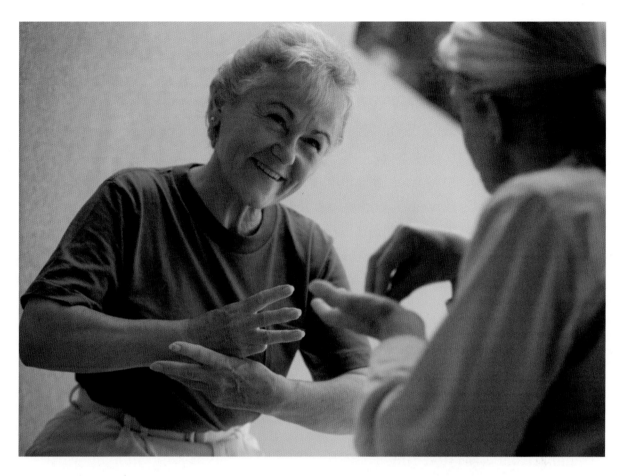

People with hearing or speech impairments may use different forms of sign language to communicate.

The five strategies include:

- Auditory-Oral: gestures, speech (lip) reading, listening with assistive devices
- Auditory-Verbal: using assistive devices to listen and speak
- Bilingual: American Sign Language, finger spelling, gestures
- Cued Speech: cueing, speech reading
- Total Communication: CASE, Manually Coded English (MCE), finger spelling, listening, speech reading, and gestures.

American Sign Language (ASL) is its own language, with its own sentence structure, grammar, and word use. It is very visual. For example, persons using ASL to ask a question will use their hands to form the question and raise their eyebrows to note that their words are a question. Parts of words are dropped for ease of use, such as endings "ed," "ing," or "ment." Many words are formed by visual displays rather than by letters, for example, the word "school" in ASL is expressed by clapping the hands together two or three times.

Finger spelling uses the hands to represent each letter of the alphabet. Although this is slower, it can give a more exact meaning. Cued speech is a method for hearing impaired people who are listening or speech reading to better understand a verbal speaker. As the speaker talks, he or she also uses finger spelling to express the first letter or two of the words they are saying.

Conceptually Accurate Signed English (CASE) is a mixture of methods and is considered to be the most precise form of communication. CASE includes visual signs from ASL, finger spelling for words not found in ASL, gestures, listening with assistive devices, speech and Manually Coded English (MCE). MCE is a form of communication that includes signs from ASL and finger spelling but uses the same grammar, word order and sentence structure as spoken English.

PROPRIOCEPTION PROBLEMS

Proprioception, sometimes called the sixth sense is the sensory information that helps the brain recognize the body's movement, gravity, balance and position. Many of the proprioception receptors are located on nerves throughout the body. Gravity and balance receptors, part of the vestibular system, are located in the inner ear. Proprioception can be damaged by viral or bacterial infections of the inner ear, the vestibular nerve, or the lining of the brain (meningitis). Head or brain injuries can also damage

If the cilia or other parts of the vestibular system are injured or damaged, a person could have trouble moving and balancing.

proprioception. Nerve disease, such as multiple sclerosis, can also impair the vestibular system and interfere with proprioception.

Symptoms of proprioception problems include dizziness, motion sickness, imbalance, disorientation, and vertigo. People with vertigo experience the sense that their surroundings are whirling around them. They often feel the sensation of being in a high place. Some people with physical and developmental disabilities have a reduced sense of proprioception. In many cases, for many people, physical and occupational therapy as well as some medication can improve their sense of balance, motion and equilibrium.

LOSS OF THE SENSE OF SMELL

Many people have temporarily experienced the loss of the sense of smell while suffering from a cold or having an allergic reaction affecting the nose. As excess mucus fills the nose and blocks the passage of air, air does not filter through the cilia in the olfactory epithelium. The receptors on the cilia cannot respond to stimuli and cannot transmit sensory information to the brain. Other causes of nasal blockages can also interfere with the receptors in the nose such as nasal polyps, which are soft growths formed on the lining of the nose, tumors, and deformities of the nasal septum.

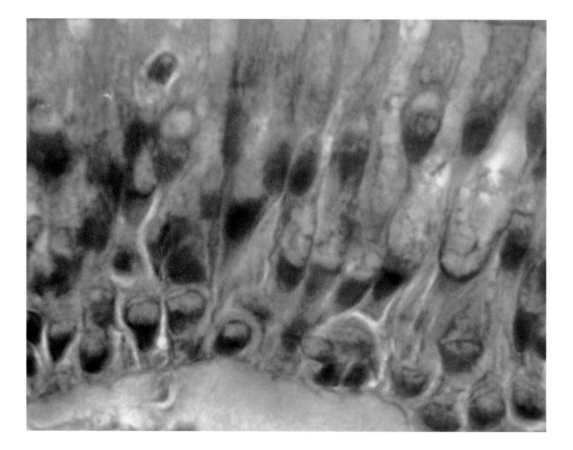

If the cells in the nasal cavity are blocked or damaged by mucus or debris, the sense of smell can be affected.

The loss of smell can also be neurological. In other words, damage to the brain or the nerves that connect to the brain from the olfactory bulb can create a loss of smell. Aging and dementia as well as certain prescription medications, including over-use of nasal decongestants, can contribute to a loss or reduction in the ability to smell. Many of those who have lost the ability to smell also lose much of their appetite or interest in foods, since the sense of smell can affect the sense of taste. A reduced sense of smell is known medically as hyposmia and an altered sense of smell is called anosmia.

LOSS OF THE SENSE OF TASTE

Losing the sense of taste is usually combined with losing the sense of smell. While the sense of taste provides information about whether foods are sweet, salty, sour, or bitter, it is the sense of smell that provides the complexity of flavors. Problems with the sense of taste come from various disorders affecting the sense of smell. Problems with taste can also be from certain medications, viral or bacterial infections that affect taste buds and the nerves leading from the mouth to the brain, head and brain injuries, diseases of the nerves such as Parkinson's or Alzheimer's, disorders affecting the production of saliva, exposure to toxic chemicals, and complications from dental or middle ear surgery.

To some who are asked the question if they had to lose one of the senses, which would it be, the answer is taste. Many people think that losing the sense of taste would not be too bad. However, the sense of taste is more than sensing flavors. It also protects people from ingesting dangerous foods and beverages, or those that may cause an allergic response. Also, loss of a sense of taste can contribute to malnutrition, obesity, and depression.

Some people experience a condition called phantageusia, or phantom tastes. This condition is caused by a disruption in brain chemistry and in

The body can sometimes repair and replace damaged taste buds, but problems with taste may be permanent.

the chemoreceptors found in taste buds. A phantom taste is an unpleasant taste that is produced by what would otherwise be a normal or appealing flavor. Hypoguesia refers to a reduced sense of taste, and aguesia refers to a total loss of taste, which is very rare.

LOSS OF THE SENSE OF TOUCH

The skin is the largest organ. It has thousands of touch receptors that convert stimuli into electrical signals to be sent to the brain. The brain then processes the information and tells the muscles and other body parts to react. Its most important duty is to inform the brain when there is danger, such as extreme temperature or pain. Somesthesia is the medical term that describes a sensory disorder that affects the sense of touch, pain, and temperature. This disorder can be a symptom of other diseases, such as the nerve disease Guillian-Barre, or the kidney disease, PKD. Some children born with developmental delays also experience a reduction or loss of the sense of touch. People who have been affected by this condition can be unsteady, can have difficulty holding onto objects and can inaccurately assess temperature, leading to burns or if too cold, hypothermia. Hypothermia is a condition in which the body temperature drops below the ability for the body to supply adequate nutrients. In extreme situations, this can result in tissue death or organ failure.

Another condition is called dysfunction of sensory integration (DSI) or sensory integration disorder (SID). People with DSI have a sense of touch that misinforms the brain of its surroundings. They can be over sensitive to sensations of touch, or under sensitive. Some examples of being over sensitive may mean that they are more ticklish than others, or feel that their clothing is unbearably itchy, or they may refuse foods because of their unpleasant-seeming textures. Objects to them may seem hotter or colder than they actually are, leading to inappropriate and sometimes dangerous responses.

Those with DSI may also be under sensitive to touch. For example, they may have a very high threshold for experiencing pain, or they may need to seek firmness or extra pressure in order to be aware of their surroundings, such as sitting in a hard chair or a rocking chair, or needing a firm grip on a pencil. Special health care providers can provide treatment, known as sensory integration therapy, for this condition. Many families also learn adaptive behaviors, such as providing soft clothing, removing the tags from inside collars, therapy balls for bouncing activities, or hard chairs to sit on.

4

Keeping the Senses Sharp

T he senses give the brain information about the body's movement and position in space and knowledge of its surroundings and the world beyond. Without them, people would stumble around unfeeling and unaware. People must attempt to live healthy lives to maintain maximum use of their senses. Each sense contributes different stimuli to the brain and each requires special care.

HEALTHY VISION

Healthy vision is dependent on two major activities: prevention and regular eye care. To prevent damage to the eye, people should take

Regular checkups with your doctor can help you stay healthy and keep your senses sharp.

Sunglasses and other protective eyewear are important whenever you go outside because the sun's rays can damage your eyes.

simple precautions to protect the eye in everyday situations. Around the house there are many occasions where liquids, household cleaners, fumes, dust particles, or other specks of debris can injure the eye. Working with tools or machinery or playing sports can also cause a sudden eye injury. Wearing safety goggles or sports goggles can prevent damage to the eyes. Most importantly, it is wise to be careful with fire and to steer clear of fireworks, while keeping in mind that sparks can also cause injury to bystanders. Excess exposure to sunlight can also damage the eyes. To protect the eyes, it is important to wear sunglasses and whenever possible, a hat with a wide brim.

At home, work, or school many people spend long periods of time staring at computer screens. This activity not only tires and dries out the eyes, but can cause episodes of blurred or double vision. Blinking often to encourage tears helps, as do some eye drop medications that lubricate the eyes. Experts also offer ideas for keeping eyes healthy while using computers, including positioning the computer screen slightly below the eyes; adjusting screen brightness and contrast; and making characters on screen much brighter than the background. People should also make

Overusing or improperly using the computer can lead to eye strain and other discomfort.

If you have glasses or contact lenses, you should wear them as prescribed by your doctor.

sure that the lights in the room should be three times brighter than the computer background. When using the computer for a long period of time, people should also take short, frequent breaks

In general, a healthy body contributes to healthy eyes. People should definitely avoid smoking. They should eat healthy, exercise, and watch their blood pressure. Vitamins A, C, E, B2, the minerals zinc and selenium, and the carotenoids lutein and zeaxanthin are particularly important to eye health. Many of these can be found in a balanced diet with plenty of fruits and green leafy vegetables, as well as foods with omega-3 fats, such as fish, nuts, squash, cooked spinach, broccoli, and beans. Omega-3 fats are not made in the body, so it is wise to include foods that contain them. Carotenoids are pigments found in many fruits and vegetables that help the body manufacture Vitamin A.

Regular eye examinations are also critical to eye health. Starting from infancy, eye examinations can help detect any problems or changes in vision. There are three types of eye specialists. Ophthalmologists are medical doctors who provide complete eye care, such as examinations, prescription lenses, surgery, and treatment for eye diseases. Optometrists are special health care providers who can perform many eye care services such as examinations and prescription lenses. He or she can diagnose some eye problems and prescribe some medications. Opticians fill prescriptions for eyeglasses and sometimes contact lenses.

An eye exam includes many procedures. Among them are a vision distance test, a peripheral vision test, a pressure test for glaucoma, an eye muscle test, and a retinal test. For this, a doctor will give eye drops to dilate the eyes (open the pupils). Once opened, he or she will shine a bright light into the interior of the eye and, by using a special scope, will inspect the retina and the optical nerve. If corrective lenses are needed, the exam will also include a series of tests to assess the best lens refraction to correct vision.

HEARING

Ears are a sensitive instrument and should be cared for with respect. Harmful noise can easily damage the inner ear. Hearing health depends on being aware of the dangers of loud noises and protecting the ears by avoiding them. Hearing loss can arise from prolonged exposure to loud noise, or from a brief, sudden explosion.

Harmful noise environments can be found nearly everywhere. Extremely loud sounds from traffic, television, rock concerts, machinery,

Listening to music at high volumes can permanently damage your ears. This is especially true when using headphones or earbuds.

jet engines, sirens, motorcycles, speedboats, chainsaws, firecrackers, lawn mowers, and leaf blowers, can all cause hearing loss. If the situation is unavoidable, a person should protect the ears with earplugs or specially made ear muffs and take short "quiet" breaks from the noise. Never try and drown out one loud sound with another, for example turning up an MP3 player because the traffic is too loud. It is also not healthy to have many loud noises going on at once—television, music, and a vacuum cleaner, for example. Experts say that whenever shouting is necessary to be heard, then the background noise is damaging.

Physicians and audiologists, who are hearing specialists, can perform hearing tests and ear examinations. These exams are especially important if people are exposed to noisy conditions on a regular basis, but people should have their hearing monitored throughout their lifetime. A

Speak quietly or whisper when you are near someone else's ears. Shouting or other loud noises can cause temporary or even permanent hearing loss.

traditional method of testing is called a pure tone threshold test. By using a sound proof cubicle, noises are introduced and the test assesses whether hearing is within normal frequency ranges. Other exams include a test to determine the ability to hear quiet speech and a test that determines the ability to hear normal speech while background noises grow increasingly louder.

There is great concern today among health professionals about the consequences of music players and headphone use. The small headphones or ear buds feed sound directly into the ear. Experts are uncertain what effects long-term use will have on hearing health in the future. Many recommend keeping the volume of the player at 50 percent of its maximum capacity.

BALANCE AND PROPRIOCEPTION

Balance and body awareness, or proprioception, rely on good vision, strong muscles, and healthy eating habits. Sports and general exercise

Exercise can help keep you fit and also helps with your balance and movements.

develop coordination, body awareness and a stronger sense of balance and equilibrium. Healthy proprioception prevents injury due to accidental falls and adds to a sense of wellbeing. There are many therapies and exercises designed to increase proprioception. Many come from traditional Eastern practices such as karate, aikido, yoga, or tai chi.

SMELLING AND TASTING

The sense of taste and smell are closely linked. Sniffing at new and pleasing fragrances or taste-testing flavorful new foods can develop new sensory receptors and keep the sense of smell and the sense of taste sharp. Maintaining a healthy sense of smell and a healthy sense of taste can be as simple as avoiding colds and other upper respiratory infections by eating a nutritious diet, exercising, and practicing good hygiene. A cold or other respiratory illness often reduces the function of olfactory and taste sensors. But after catching a cold or other respiratory illness, the senses of smell and taste usually return on their own, though it may be gradual.

Sometimes the sense of smell or the sense of taste are affected by prescription medications. It is important to mention to health care providers whenever there is a loss of smell or taste. Often, an alternate medication can be given. Some studies have shown that certain trace minerals may play a role in keeping the proteins responsible for taste and olfactory cell growth healthy, such as copper, zinc, calcium, and magnesium.

A HEALTHY SENSE OF TOUCH

The sense of touch comes from millions of sensory receptors imbedded in the skin. Skin is made up of many layers, and new skin cells are being made all the time and push dead cells to the top layer where they are worn away. Keeping the body well nourished and supplied with plenty of water helps the skin stay healthy. It is also important to protect the skin from

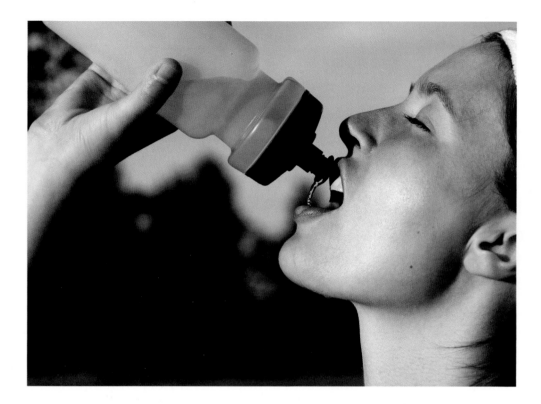

Drinking the right amount of fluids provides your body with the nutrients it needs to function properly.

too much exposure to the sun. People who do a lot of rough work with their hands, or go barefoot outdoors develop harder, thicker skin, called calluses, on their hands and feet. Calluses interfere with the sense of touch, making sensation more difficult and preventing the receptors from detecting texture, temperature, and pain. Oils and creams can help soften the skin and restore the ability of the skin to respond to touch stimuli.

The sense of touch can also be improved upon by simply recognizing the feedback from touch receptors. For example, enjoying the feel of diving into cool, clean water on a hot afternoon or appreciating a soft pillow after a long, tiring day. Giving a friend a hug or holding someone's hand when crossing a busy street also produces positive responses from touch

Keeping your skin clean and moisturized is one easy way to help protect your sense of touch.

sensations. Such experiences can boost levels of wellbeing and prime the body to react more often and more thoroughly to new touch stimuli.

The senses respond to the body's environment and present the brain with vital information. Billions of nerve cells react to sensory stimuli and transmit impulses that help defend the body from danger, pain, and harm. Sensory receptors almost instantaneously give the brain the ability to identify people and objects, to listen to music and sounds, to maintain balance and equilibrium, to distinguish textures and temperature, and to smell aromas and feast on favorite foods. The human senses are the means to experience the world and their many complexities are extraordinary.

Glossary

action potential—An electrical impulse discharged by neurons.

aguesia—The loss of the sense of taste.

anosmia—A lack of sense of smell.

aqueous humor—The fluid between the cornea and the lens of the eye.

astigmatism—A condition in which the lens of the eye is irregularly curved, causing out of focus images.

axon—The tail of a neuron or nerve cell that emits electrical impulses.

cataract—A cloudy covering that occurs over the lens of the eye.

cerumen—Ear wax.

chemoreceptor—Sensory receptor that responds to chemical stimuli.

circumvallate papillae—Projections on the surface of the tongue that contain taste buds.

cochlea—A spiral-shaped cavity in the inner ear that contains the receptors for hearing in the organ of Corti.

Conceptually Accurate Signed English (CASE)—A form of communication that includes hand signs, speech reading, speaking, and cued English.

conchae—Bony ridges that allow passage of air in the nose.

cones—Photoreceptors in the retina of the eye that detect colors.

cornea—The transparent front portion of the sclera of the eye.

decibel—The measure of the loudness of sound.

dilate—To open something wider, such as the pupils.

Dysfunction of Sensory Integration (DSI)—A disorder of the sense of touch, in which people may be over or under sensitive.

fovea—The center of the retina where vision is the most acute.

fungiform papillae—Projections found all over the tongue that contain taste buds.

glossopharyngeal nerve—The nerve that carries taste information from the back of the tongue to the brain.

glaucoma—A vision disorder that involves the build-up of pressure behind the eye..

gustation—The sense of taste.

hertz—The measure of the frequency of sound in cycles per second.

hyperopia—Farsightedness, which means that objects that are farther away are clearer.

hypoguesia—A reduced sense of taste.

hyposmia—A reduced sense of smell.

incus—One of the ossicles of the middle ear, known commonly as the anvil.

iris—The pigmented ring of muscles that surround the pupil.

lingual papillae—Bumps on the tongue that contain taste buds.

macula—The center of the retina.

macular degeneration—A retinal disease that can lead to blindness.

malleus—One of the ossicles of the middle ear, known commonly as the hammer.

mechanoreceptors— A sensory receptor that responds to pressure stimuli.

myopia—Nearsightedness, which means that objects are clearer when they are closer.

neurotransmitter—A chemical messenger within the body.

nociceptor—A pain receptor.

olfactory—Having to do with the sense of smell.

optic chiasma—An area where the nerves leading from each eye meet and cross.

optic disk—A blind spot, or area in the back of the eye where the optic nerve passes through.

organ of corti—A mass of tiny hairs that are the hearing receptors.

ossicles—The tiniest bones in the body found in the middle ear that help amplify sound.

pinna—The outer ear, which is sometimes also called the auricle.

proprioception—The "sixth sense" based in the inner ear that provides the brain with information about the body's position in space, balance, and equilibrium.

retina— The back of the eye.

rod—A photoreceptor in the retina of the eye that detects dim light.

semicircular canals—The chambers in the middle ear.

stapes—One of the ossicles of the middle ear, known commonly as the stirrups.

thalamus—A part of the brain that processes and relays sensory information to the cerebral cortex of the brain.

vestibulocochlear nerve—The nerve that leads from the inner ear to the brain that provides sensory information from the ear.

visual cortex—The area of the brain responsible for processing visual information.

vitreous humor—The jelly-like fluid found behind the lens of the eye.

Find Out More

Books

Dunn, Winnie. *Living Sensationally: Understanding Your Senses.*
   Philadelphia: Jessica Kingsley Publishers, 2008.

Light, Douglas B. *The Senses.* Philadelphia, PA: Chelsea House, 2005.

Mayo Clinic. *Mayo Clinic on Vision and Eye Health.* Rochester, MN: Mayo
   Clinic Health Information, 2002.

Websites

American Speech-Language-Hearing Association (ASHA)
   http://www.asha.org

**Howard Hughes Medical Institute: A Report on Seeing, Hearing and
   Smelling the World.**
   http://www.hhmi.org/senses/

Lighthouse International Headquarters
   http://www.lighthouse.org

National Association of the Deaf
   http://www.nad.org/

Neuroscience for Kids
http://faculty.washington.edu/chudler/chsense.html

Index

Page numbers in **boldface** are illustrations.

About the Author

Ruth Bjorklund lives on Bainbridge Island, across Puget Sound from Seattle, Washington. She lives with her husband, daughter, son, four dogs, and a cat. She has written several books for young people about human health and anatomy and found research into the human senses fascinating.